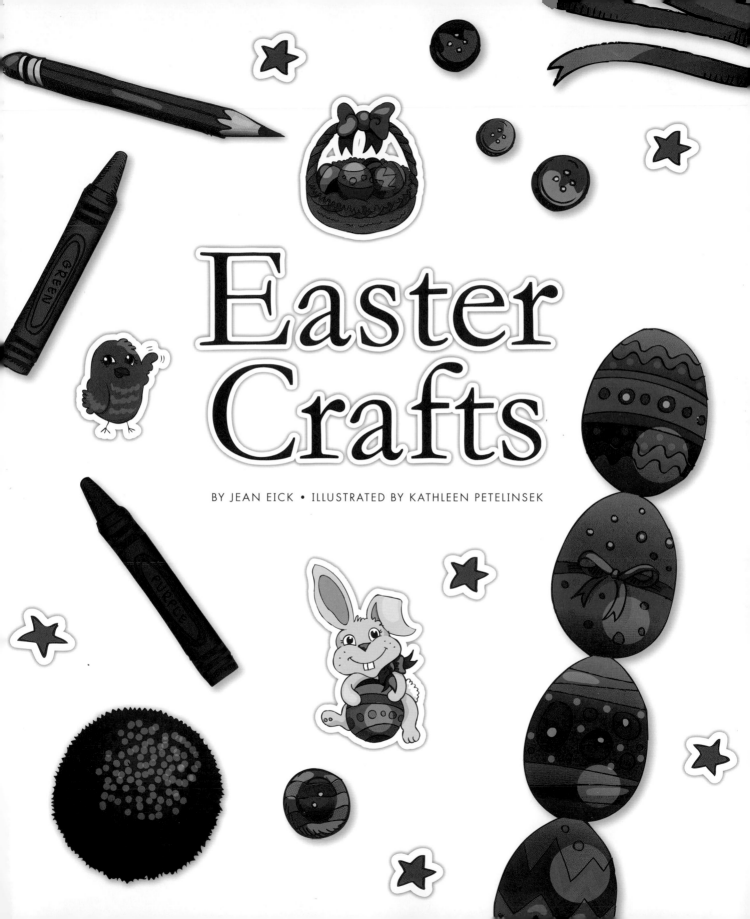

Easter Crafts

BY JEAN EICK • ILLUSTRATED BY KATHLEEN PETELINSEK

Published by The Child's World®
1980 Lookout Drive
Mankato, MN 56003-1705
800-599-READ
www.childsworld.com

The Child's World®: Mary Berendes, Publishing Director
The Design Lab: Design and production

Library of Congress Cataloging-in-Publication Data
Eick, Jean, 1947–
  Easter crafts / by Jean Eick; illustrated by Kathleen Petelinsek.
     p. cm.
  ISBN 978-1-60954-233-7 (library bound: alk. paper)
  1. Easter decorations–Juvenile literature. 2. Handicraft–Juvenile
literature. I. Petelinsek, Kathleen, ill. II. Title.
  TT900.E2E352 2011
  745.594'1667–dc22   2010035495

Printed in the United States of America
Mankato, MN
February, 2012
PA02129

Table of Contents

Happy Easter!

Easter is a special **holiday** for many people around the world. On this day, **Christians** celebrate the day Jesus Christ rose from the dead. Many people also celebrate new life and new beginnings. Easter's date changes every year, but it is always on a Sunday in spring.

People have celebrated Easter for over a thousand years. In many **cultures**, it's a time to be with family and friends. Many people go to church. Some families bake special breads and meats. Often, eggs are used in Easter celebrations. Eggs have long been a **symbol** of new life. At Easter time, people decorate eggs, have egg hunts, and even make yummy egg recipes!

Let's Begin!

1 This book is full of great ideas you can make to celebrate Easter. There are ideas for decorations, gifts, and cards. There are activities at the end of this book, too!

2 Before you start making any craft, be sure to read the **directions**. Make sure you look at the pictures too—they will help you understand what to do. Go through the list of things you'll need and get everything together. When you're ready, find a good place to work. Now you can begin making your crafts!

Paper Eggs

You can make lots of pretty eggs to put up almost anywhere.

THINGS YOU'LL NEED

Scissors

Construction paper (light colors are best)

Pencil

Ribbon

Buttons

Glitter

Markers and crayons

Glue

Stickers

DIRECTIONS

1 Use your pencil to draw an egg shape on a piece of construction paper.

2 Carefully cut out the egg with your scissors.

3 Decorate the egg any way you'd like! Here are some ideas:
- Use glue and glitter to make a sparkly egg.
- Use crayons and markers to make a colorful, arty egg.
- Use stickers, ribbons, and even buttons to make an extra-special egg.

Egg Strings

Egg strings are fun to hang along walls.

THINGS YOU'LL NEED

Scissors

Construction paper (light colors are best)

Pencil

A cookie-cutter shaped like an egg

Ribbon

Buttons

Glitter

Markers and crayons

Glue

Stickers

1 Use the pencil to trace around the cookie-cutter. Then trace another egg shape right above it (don't leave any space!). Then trace another egg shape above that one. Your paper should have room for three or four eggs.

2 Fold the paper back and forth. Make sure the first fold is just a little bit shorter than the egg shape's top and bottom edges. As you fold, be sure the edges of the paper line up.

3 Carefully cut out the egg shape. Remember not to cut through the folded areas!

4 Open the folds and you'll see a chain of connected eggs. Decorate any way you'd like. Then hang up your egg string wherever you think it would look nice.

Bunny

These cute bunnies are fun when they move in the breeze.

THINGS YOU'LL NEED

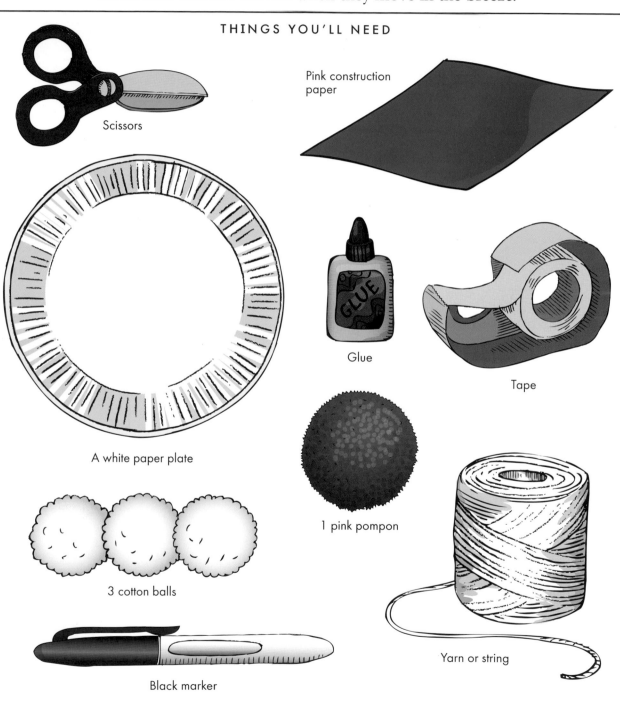

Scissors

Pink construction paper

A white paper plate

Glue

Tape

1 pink pompon

3 cotton balls

Yarn or string

Black marker

DIRECTIONS

1 Use the marker to draw a bunny face on the plate.

2 Glue the pompon on the plate to make the bunny's nose. Glue the cotton balls on the plate to make the bunny's mouth area.

3 Cut out two bunny-ear shapes from the construction paper.

4 Glue the ears to the back of the plate. Tape a piece of yarn or string to the back of the plate, too.

5 Hang your happy bunny anywhere you'd like!

Bunny Basket

These baskets make nice Easter surprises for your teachers and friends.

THINGS YOU'LL NEED

Scissors

Glue

2 pink pompons

Yarn or string

Pink construction paper

Brown paper bag

Pencil

Black marker

DIRECTIONS

1 Use the pencil to draw bunny ears halfway down on all four corners of the bag.

2 Carefully cut along the lines.

3 Use the black marker to draw a bunny face. Be sure to make some whiskers!

4 With the pencil, draw two bunny-ear shapes on the pink paper. Cut out the pink ear shapes.

5 Glue the ear shapes on the two front ears. Glue the 2 pompons to the front of the bag to make the bunny's mouth area.

6 Tie the front and back ears together with the string or yarn. Fill the basket with pretty tissue paper and Easter candy!

Egg Holders

These holders are a great way to show off your Easter eggs.

THINGS YOU'LL NEED

Toilet-paper tube

Scissors

Glue

Ribbon

Stickers for decorating

Crayons or markers

Wrapping paper

DIRECTIONS

1 Lay the toilet-paper tube flat. Use your scissors to cut it in half.

2 Decorate the tube with your crayons and markers. Or you can put stickers on it. Or you can cut pieces of wrapping paper and glue them onto your tube. Be creative!

3 Carefully place an Easter egg on top of the holder.

Easter Cards

Many people like to send Easter cards to their friends and family. Now you can make your own cards.

THINGS YOU'LL NEED

Scissors

Construction paper (lots of different colors)

Glitter

Glue

Ribbon

Buttons

Pencil

Crayons, markers, or paint

Stickers or magazine pictures

DIRECTIONS FOR CARD ONE

1 Fold a piece of construction paper to the size you want it to be. Folding once will make a large card. Folding it twice will make a smaller card.

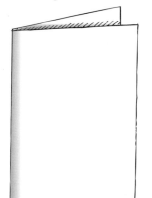

2 Decorate the front of the card any way you'd like. You can use ribbons, buttons, glitter, and stickers—be creative! Write a message on the inside of the card. You can decorate the inside, too. Don't forget to sign your name!

DIRECTIONS FOR CARD TWO

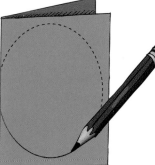

1 Instead of making a square card, make one shaped like an egg! Use your pencil to draw an egg shape on a folded piece of paper. Remember, one edge of the egg must hang over the folded part of the paper!

2 Cut out the shape with your scissors.

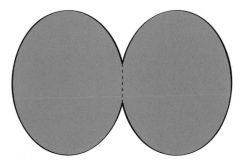

3 Now open the card. You should see two eggs!

4 Decorate the card however you'd like. You can even use pictures from magazines that remind you of Easter. Some ideas are flowers, baby animals, and sunshine.

Envelopes

You can make your own envelopes to fit your homemade cards.

THINGS YOU'LL NEED

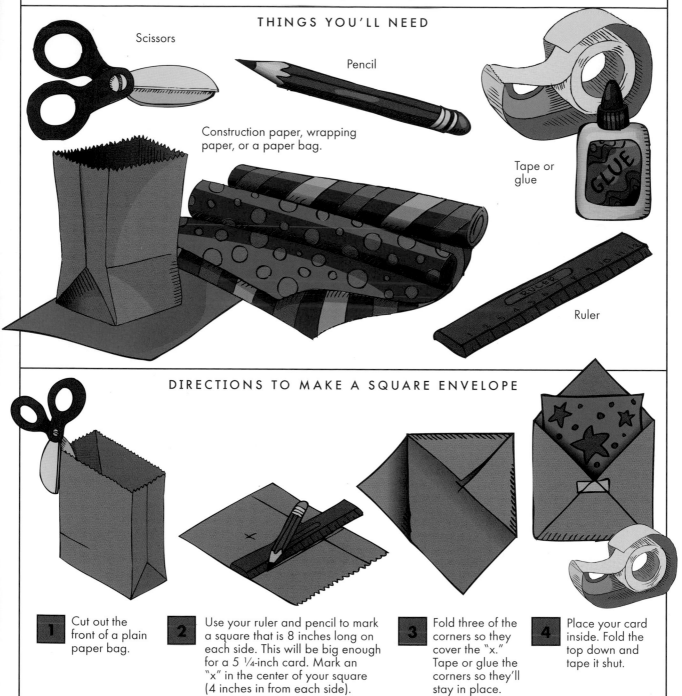

Scissors

Pencil

Construction paper, wrapping paper, or a paper bag.

Tape or glue

GLUE

Ruler

DIRECTIONS TO MAKE A SQUARE ENVELOPE

1 Cut out the front of a plain paper bag.

2 Use your ruler and pencil to mark a square that is 8 inches long on each side. This will be big enough for a 5 ¼-inch card. Mark an "x" in the center of your square (4 inches in from each side).

3 Fold three of the corners so they cover the "x." Tape or glue the corners so they'll stay in place.

4 Place your card inside. Fold the top down and tape it shut.

DIRECTIONS TO MAKE AN ENVELOPE THAT'S NOT SQUARE

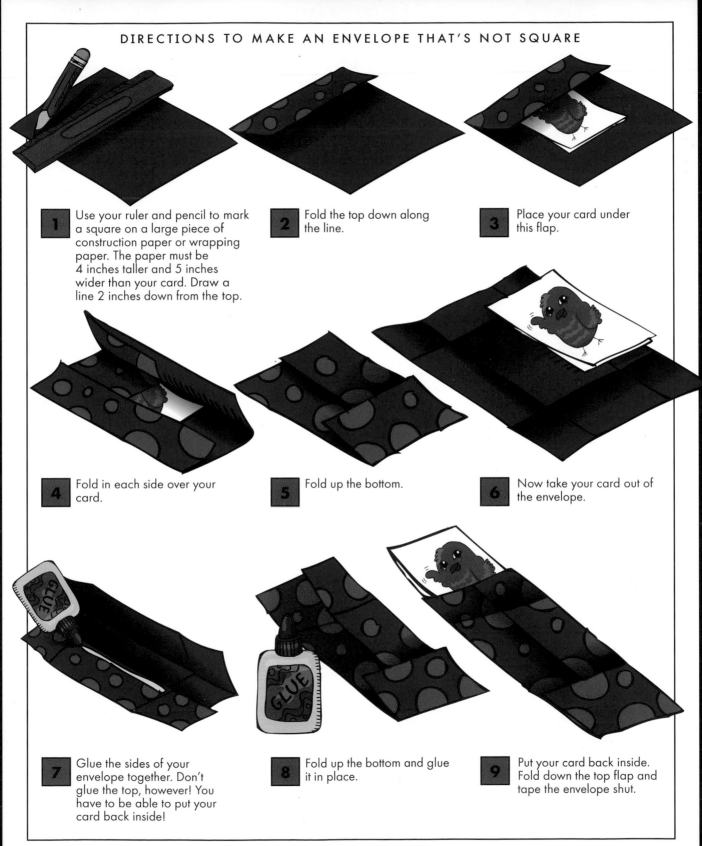

1 Use your ruler and pencil to mark a square on a large piece of construction paper or wrapping paper. The paper must be 4 inches taller and 5 inches wider than your card. Draw a line 2 inches down from the top.

2 Fold the top down along the line.

3 Place your card under this flap.

4 Fold in each side over your card.

5 Fold up the bottom.

6 Now take your card out of the envelope.

7 Glue the sides of your envelope together. Don't glue the top, however! You have to be able to put your card back inside!

8 Fold up the bottom and glue it in place.

9 Put your card back inside. Fold down the top flap and tape the envelope shut.

Activities

There are many things you can do with others to celebrate Easter. Here are some fun ideas.

1 Have an egg-decorating party! Invite your friends over to decorate some **hard-boiled** eggs an adult has cooked for you. Have each person bring something to decorate the eggs, such as crayons or stickers.

2 Start a garden. Plant some seeds in a pot or small container. Water the seeds and give them plenty of sunlight. When the seeds have sprouted, take them outside and plant them in the ground to grow!

3 Have an Easter parade. Wear fancy hats and dress up with your friends. Then show your parents how nice you look.

4 Have an egg-and-spoon race. In your yard, have everyone stand side-by-side. Give everyone a spoon. Then give everyone a hard-boiled egg (be sure it's still in the shell). Have everyone place their egg on their spoon. Then race! The winner is the first person to get to the finish line without dropping the egg off the spoon.

Glossary

directions (dir-EK-shunz) Directions are the steps for how to do something. You should follow the directions in this book to make your crafts.

hard-boiled (HARD BOYLD) A hard-boiled egg is one that has been cooked in its shell. Hard boiled eggs are firm instead of gooey.

holiday (HOL-uh-day) A holiday is a time for celebration, such as Christmas or Valentine's Day. Easter is a holiday.

symbol (SIM-bull) A symbol is an object that stands for something else. Eggs are a symbol of new life.

Find More Crafts

BOOKS

Ross, Kathy, and Sharon Lane Holm (illustrator). *All New Crafts for Easter*. Brookfield, CT: Millbrook Press, 2004.

Stamper, Judith Bauer, and Julie Durrell (illustrator). *Easter Fun Activity Book*. Mahwah, NJ: Troll Associates, 1997.

WEB SITES

Visit our Web site for links to more crafts: childsworld.com/links

Note to Parents, Teachers, and Librarians: We routinely verify our Web links to make sure they are safe and active sites. So encourage your readers to check them out!

Index

activities, 22

baskets, 14

bunnies, 12, 14

cards, 18

celebrating, 4, 5

Christians, 4

cultures, 5

date, 4

egg holders, 16

eggs, 5, 8, 10, 16, 22

envelopes, 18

holiday, 4

Jesus Christ, 4

new life, 4

spring, 4

strings, 10

ABOUT THE AUTHOR

Jean Eick has written over 200 books for children over the past forty years. She has written biographies, craft books, and many titles on nature and science. Jean lives in Lake Tahoe with her husband and enjoys hiking in the mountains, reading, and doing volunteer work.